DEC 3 0 2002

Independence Day

by Helen Frost

Consulting Editor: Gail Saunders-Smith, Ph.D.
Consultant: Alexa Sandmann, Ed.D.
Professor of Literacy
The University of Toledo
Member, National Council for the Social Studies

Pebble Books

an imprint of Capstone Press
Mankato, Minnesota

Pebble Books are published by Capstone Press
151 Good Counsel Drive, P.O. Box 669, Mankato, Minnesota 56002
http://www.capstone-press.com

1 2 3 4 5 6 05 04 03 02 01 00

Library of Congress Cataloging-in-Publication Data
Frost, Helen, 1949–
    Independence Day/by Helen Frost.
    p. cm.—(National holidays)
    Includes bibliographical references and index.
    Summary: Simple text and photographs explain Independence Day, how and
why we celebrate it to honor the founding of the United States.
    ISBN 0-7368-0542-7
    1. Fourth of July—Juvenile literature. 2. Fourth of July celebrations—Juvenile
literature. [1. Fourth of July. 2. Holidays.] I. Title. II. Series.
E286.A1294   2000
394.26'0973—dc21   99-049389

Note to Parents and Teachers

The National Holidays series supports national social studies
standards related to understanding events that celebrate the
values and principles of American democracy. This book describes
and illustrates Independence Day. The photographs support early
readers in understanding the text. This book also introduces early
readers to subject-specific vocabulary words, which are defined in
the Words to Know section. Early readers may need assistance to
read some words and to use the Table of Contents, Words to
Know, Read More, Internet Sites, and Index/Word List sections
of the book.

Table of Contents

July						
S	M	T	W	T	F	S
						1
2	3	4	5	6	7	8
9	10	11	12	13	14	15
16	17	18	19	20	21	22
23	24	25	26	27	28	29
30	31					

4

Americans celebrate Independence Day every year on July 4. They remember how the United States of America became a free country.

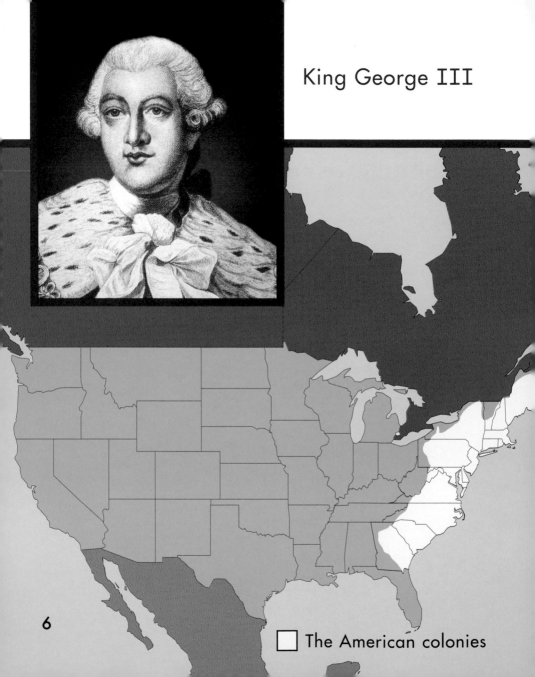

King George III

The American colonies

Great Britain once ruled America. King George III was the leader of Great Britain. He made laws for the 13 American colonies.

8

The American colonists wanted to govern their own land. They talked about fighting for their freedom. The colonies and Great Britain began to fight the Revolutionary War in 1775.

Declaration of
Independence

10

Leaders from the colonies gathered during the war. They signed the Declaration of Independence on July 4, 1776. This paper said the colonies wanted to be a free country. But Great Britain continued to fight the colonists.

The colonists won the Revolutionary War in 1783. The colonies became a free country. Colonial leaders named their new country the United States of America.

14

Americans celebrate their freedom every year on Independence Day. People also call this holiday America's birthday or the Fourth of July.

Families and friends celebrate Independence Day. They have picnics.

Communities celebrate Independence Day. They have parades.

People watch fireworks at night. Fireworks are an Independence Day tradition.

Words to Know

celebrate—to do something fun on a special occasion

colonist—a person who comes from another country and settles in a new area

colony—an area that has been settled by people from another country; a colony is ruled by another country.

Declaration of Independence—a paper declaring the freedom of the 13 American colonies from the rule of Great Britain; Thomas Jefferson wrote the Declaration of Independence; it was approved on July 4, 1776.

independence—freedom; people who are independent make decisions for themselves.

tradition—a custom, idea, or belief that is passed down through time

Read More

Dalgliesh, Alice. *The Fourth of July Story.* New York: Aladdin, 1995.

Hoig, Stan. *It's the Fourth of July!* New York: Cobblehill Books, 1995.

Merrick, Patrick. *Fourth of July Fireworks.* Chanhassen, Minn.: Child's World, 2000.

Internet Sites

Colonial Hall: A Look at America's Founders
http://www.colonialhall.com

The Fourth of July Page
http://wilstar.com/holidays/july4.htm

Independence Day on the Net
http://www.holidays.net/independence

Why Do We Celebrate the 4th of July?
http://www.kidsdomain.com/holiday/july4/why.html

23

Index/Word List

Word Count: 182
Early-Intervention Level: 18

Editorial Credits
Mari C. Schuh, editor; Heather Kindseth, cover designer; Linda Clavel, illustrator; Kimberly Danger, photo researcher

Photo Credits
Archive Photos, 6, 8, 10, 12
David F. Clobes, 20
International Stock/Scott Barrow, 1, Bobbe Wolf, 14
Spectrum Photographics/David F. Clobes Stock Photography, 18
Unicorn Stock Photos/Robin Rudd, 4, 16

24